AF413587

NUBIAN VOICES UNMASKED

An Anthology

Scripted Visions Publishing Group Presents

NUBIAN VOICES UNMASKED

An Anthology

By

NADIA STOKES, HENRY WESTRAY JR., & JOSLYN CALDWELL

For more information about the authors and Scripted Visions
Publishing Group, visit: www.scriptedvisionspublishing.com

<u>FOREWORD</u>

"The Art of Creative Collaboration"

It's a beautiful thing to witness uber-talented individuals set aside their egos, endure the required amount of sacrifice and compromise, overcome adversity, and combine their individual talents to give birth to something as beautiful, cohesive, and thought-provoking as *Nubian Voices Unmasked.*

Is there any other form of writing more pure, more authentic, and more revealing than poetry? I suppose the answer is up for debate, but what can't be disputed is the timelessness of poetry; its roots running wide and deep, stretching their way throughout time and across all cultures and geographic locations. Poetry is a truth serum and a healing salve, a written form of therapy for both the writer and the reader.

I don't remember exactly when the idea of publishing a poetry anthology first entered my mind and took hold, but I do know I have long desired to participate in a work of art like *Nubian Voices Unmasked.* And as God would have it, after this idea began as nothing more than me thinking, "Man, this would be cool to do", this project began to take shape and the pieces fell into place one by one. What started as just another entry on my long and growing "writing and publishing wish-list" has finally come to fruition.

It has been an honor and a blessing to know The Nubian Voices; first as individuals, and now as a collective creative force. I had the privilege of meeting Nadia, Henry, and Joslyn at separate times in my life. Nadia and I worked in the same office once upon a time. It was impossible not to be awestruck by her unwavering Faith, kindness, tolerance, and abundance of talent in…like…everything. So, she had to be part of this project. There was no other way. Henry and I connected through the Black Writers' Guild of Maryland. His genuine love of life and the craft of writing along with his prolific skill are traits other writers (including me) crave. It was easy to see that he would make a great contributor to this project. I met Joslyn on California's beautiful Central Coast at the wedding of a mutual friend. Someone read one of Joslyn's poems during the ceremony and the intensity, unabashed honesty, and lyrical flow of her words spoke to me and the wedding's attendees. I knew then that I wanted to work with her.

This project started as nothing more than a seed planted in my mind and heart. Now, after watering that seed with Faith, talent, and patience and after battling through a pandemic and other challenges, *Nubian Voices Unmasked* is finally here for your reading pleasure.

While not for the faint of heart, creative collaboration is an opportunity meant to be seized, savored, and maximized. Nadia, Henry, and Joslyn have embodied this sentiment. I hope and pray their words speak to your soul as they have spoken to mine. Please enjoy.

Peace and blessings,

Tyrone M. Eddins Jr.
CEO & Founder
Scripted Visions Publishing Group

NUBIAN VOICES UNMASKED

An Anthology

For out of the abundance of the heart, the mouth speaketh
-Matthew 12:34

"Dreams are themes we build our days to greet"

"The mind, the heart, the hands together make dreams into reality"

DEDICATIONS

I dedicate this book to The One who gave me life, a story, an experience to share even in the silence. All so that we know, remember, that we're not alone, someone does care, and the world truly does not revolve around us though it does involve us. We each are purposely made for a purpose. To all my brothers and sisters, mothers, and misters, of this world and next, speak life to deaden lies. Thank God for you, we. We up in here! We still growing and blood still flowing.

- NAStokes

I want to thank the many unsung heroes on whose shoulders, I stood with my head above water. They provided a safe and loving harbor from which to view the world and write what I see and feel through poetry. Their enthusiasm for wanting other people to hear my voice, makes me hope that my words will resonate with you too. As a poet, I can't find words that can truly express my heartfelt gratitude for their generous support. I would be remiss if I did not salute my dear village of friends with affection. They include: Iris Reeves, Michael Jones, Dr. Robert Smith, Jacqueline Nerette, William Thompson, Dr. Maurice Dorsey, Dr. Burney Hollis, Barbara Johnson, Charles Nixon, Carlton Cromwell, Anne Marie Lombardi, Dr. Lois Gaskins, Lipton McKain, Valerie Lee, Gwendolyn Lloyd, Dianne Russum, Corinda Jones, Celia Williams, Tyrone Eddins Jr., Nadia Stokes, Jocelyn Caldwell, Brenda Baer, Nancy Rothman, Esta Baker, Angela Adams, Shoshana Harris, Wilma Brockington-Parker, Dee Lawrence, Dr. Deborah Prothro-Stith, Dr. Marco Merrick, and the late Billye Turner and Lee Moody.

Last, I would also like to thank my family and the following organizations: The Literary Ten Book Club, The Black Writers Guild,

The Reminiscing Club, The Baltimore Senior Network, Towson
University's Osher Poetry group, The Black Mental Health Alliance,
The Harvard Field Notes Journal, The Loch Raven Review, The
Myerberg Center, Staff at Enoch Pratt Free Library, and Kimberly
Casey Collins at Cre8tive 'Kimestray"
- H.Westray, Jr

To my sons, who show me unconditional love and are everything I
could hope for and more. To those who feel like they are screaming in
a soundproof room, alone and longing to be accepted; I hope you find
comfort in our words. I am so blessed to be a writer in this collective
and it is an honor to share such an experience with Nadia and Henry.
- J Caldwell

CONTENTS

<u>INTRODUCTION</u>

Three individuals, three lives, three stories meeting in this sacred space where expression is prized, truth is honored, and creativity is housed. There is no present without the past and no growth without cultivation. We create because we've been created. We live because we've been given life. We express because we were spoken into existence. Here, in this space, we're free, kissed by the sun and bare faced. We're free because our ancestors, families, friends, mentors and even opposers both intentionally and unintentionally fought before us, with us, for us. It is our time now to continue to do the same. Spoken word, silent songs of fallen and rising souls untamed. During this time where space is unlimited, emotions are high and visions of varied mental states of our brothers and sisters of the world have come to be showcased on every form of media, we collectively stand as one for life, three spirits combined and unmasked. Silent no more. Hidden no more. Enter our world and stay for a while. Explore.
Blessings.

NADIA STOKES

I am a child of God
Creating because I was created
Living because I've been given life
Loving because I'm loved
Still undergoing renovations
I'm looking forward
Continued growth on the many levels
Sharing the testimonies
The challenges, the battles
The successes, the healing
All while nervous but with hopeful expectation
Contemplation is close to me
Dreams even closer
Humbled by reality in reach
Self-seen in each
Joining hands of creation
Forward in spite of much because of The One who is bigger than it all

Nadia Stokes, Henry Westray Jr., & Joslyn Caldwell

I've been blessed to experience this place and these kindred beings, great and small
I'm grateful and will continue as expected
The One who knows the end and beginning loves me
And you Equally, we're Never neglected
We all are an expression of God's love
Meant to share it through our gifts
This is one of mine.

<u>Aged Wisdom</u>

Is it me or does the light shine upon solely your
face as you turn towards yesterday's news?
Without knowledge of futures arriving too soon
And if it isn't, then I have eyes opened by
Spirit's work on you
And the flashing lights pass by
And worlds apart, but close in reach,
are the beings of you and I
Look through peripherals at you sir, you.

Every Day is a Dream

I saw skies that were pink
Before and I would think
That you were
An angel who'd come down to
Save me from sadness
I've watched rivers flow and
I'd think of you as a goddess
Who'd help me escape from madness
I absorbed the moonlight's shine
As I thought of you as a queen
Of hearts filled with gladness
And of all of these
Is the reality
That you are all three and my mother
And there can't be another
I'm blessed by you
Thank God for your happiness
As it's been a part of my joy

Above

Signs
Signals
Signaled
Sands to sound
    And rounded up
    Rounds

    Of ringers
    Who rang

      The voice to
        Command

Choices made
To help us stand

    And world
      Go round
        About.

Open to speak amongst the ears
Of those with shut tight mouths.

<u>Fly on the Wall</u>

I thought of you
When the snow fell
Yesterday
I dreamt of fireplaces
With your body
Lying
In front of its window
Your smile
As I walked by
On the outside
Looking in at you
Unaware
Of the sun
Warming my exposed
Shoulder
Leaned upon the glass
Beautiful was its
Description
Familiar was yours
Crackling fire was
Connection made
As you continue lying
Upon the pillowed floor

#4

Wave at me
While the sun
Drives by
Open the window
Shutters hide
Wind be good to me
Dust rise high
Water wash skin
Sins away from I
Till time tries
Fly
Again.

<u>Question</u>

Proposition was forever
Whether weather was stormy
Or filled with light
Shine upon head of two
Only eternity remains
And flower drifted petals
Can count the number twice
Of loves and nots
Till digits lack matter
Forever more
Not forever
More

<u>*Around ½*</u>

Streets with bars
Cars with windows
Lights with shadows
Nights with dreams
Bridge connections
Separation
Skewed notations
Unwoven seams
High beams from
Visions of skies
Made blue from
Airtight vacuums
Differences in
Opposition
H2O malfunction
Junction
Breath remains
Stench of toxins
Buried in the skins
Movement upward
Dead-end streets
Those made stuck
But what then?

<u>Le Chaise</u>

Spoke of a song
Sang about a chaise
Made of trees
Of the Congo
Representative of
Companies kept
In neighborhoods
Shaken by segregated
Ideologies of
The lawmaking
Philosophical ones
BIG was its name
Is- only Monument
For sight
Captured
Held amongst
Hostages of
Gentrification
Repeated days
To sing again
And radio destroyed
Humming melodies
Of old lady in Oak DC

Light Being

Gritted milk of
Mud hoofed beings
Taken up upon the rafters
Ceilings...and sun
Come down in form
Of leanings- human
Goddess being- truth
Spoken loud- in a
Thunderous storm
Dirt just flying
Life is born- whirlwinds
Settling as clouds grow white
Word filled being...you beam light

Perceptive "Non lies"

Spoken truth based upon
Notions of words heard
Displayed the wrong way
Understanding
Twisted by
Shut ears- unbeknownst to
The teller of stories and lessons
Prescribed by light.
Utilized for
Movement and lack of might.
For clarity was stricken by screens
Made cloud and truths of absolute
Turned lies out loud...Miss, under, stood.

__Renaissance__

I told you earlier that I was sorry for what I've
done to you
For neglecting you, for always trying to perfect
the perfect in you
For letting you down
For putting you there
For putting others before you
Before God
The most important beings in both of our lives
I told you that I didn't know at the time
That I was
Not myself
I was changing
To rearrange placements not meant for us to stay
Because we were swayed by the idea of
Love
Not its truth
The idea
Implanted by fantasies
Romantic comedies
Of reality
Distorted
By past pain
When I said I was sorry I meant it,
I do
I love you so
So much I love you
Like that of God,

No one should ever be above you
Will never be above you
But God
We won't settle for less
Than what The Most High proclaimed
Suggested, Says
In numerous books, signs, tears
Look at me… no…look at you
We are the same…better
Made for
God's
Meant to be light, free
I promise you, I'll never let you hurt me, we
again
It would break the heart of The One who loves
us the same
I could never live with that blame again
Though no shame with The Creator who we
deem Him
I just won't live that way again
Light too bright to let it dim
Thank you so much for your forgiveness
I'm so proud of you. I'm in love with you
The love within you brightens my day, I smile at
you, you smile at me
We together for the ever always
I'm the light in you too
Settling, never again, for we too high not to win.
You, me, we, I am.
Stop…Begin.

<u>Water will fall</u>

Look at that sky
Its windows are so clear and triumphant
In its brightness
In its warmth
In its vastness
In its haunting manner
Beaming above and simultaneously
All around

Breathe in the breeze that eases our facial hairs
Light and dark and hot and stark
And naked we lay above our former selves
Reaching high on shelves created by mountain
peaks of the plates
That chose to meet at a place
To beseech
Those who search and those who teach
But wait
Sun never set; we just tilt our heads to see the
varying light

Surrounded by the love unspoken of
Take flight
Bye bye pumpkin pie
I see you tonight
When we move again in quarter time
Trusting that when we open our eyes
We'll see the light again

Never-ending cycling of spinning waters
are our friends
And music, sweet sounds of chirping and waves
and breathing, shallow voices
Of memories, fading and engaging solar plexus
Complexities broken up to see
The sea is forever going, even below the ground
Where the seeds grow
Fruit soon to be tasted…now found
They fall and they come up again

<u>*Not Completely Different*</u>

We're not completely different,
We're just different versions of ourselves.
When we started, life's happenings to us and
around us began to change our ways,
Our true truth,
 And we adapted, adopted
  And became what we thought was us
 Or what we were told was.
 We walked in it forgetting the
 Beginning.
Then we wore a covering of a self not born
          But something happens when we resee our
form
And then we choose to become a newer version
of ourselves,
Back to what was meant
 But we have to choose to do so.
If we want to ever fly,
We have to go through metamorphosis because
we can't be caterpillars all our lives.
 Keep in mind that there's still a caterpillar in a
butterfly.
 Same, just grown
 And the transition takes time.
 It becomes automatic when we know the need.
Like caterpillars
We have to rest in a cocoon of self after having
been born

And exposed to
And a part of
Surrounding life,
Then we transform to greater heights.
Without those needed steps,
Caterpillars end where they were left,
Stuck to a leaf,
Leaving without their destined wings.

Sometimes

I got to tell you this story
About this girl; this girl…she's a woman now
Realizes she's not really of this world
Paralyzed by confusion in the midst of truth
Once before now
But she's been given the opportunity to walk
forward now
And so she said, "ok, I'll do it"
Nothing to it
Inside a little afraid
Outside she seemed brave
Was actually because she was going to do it
Nothing to it
So she went and she sat down and she thought
and she fell asleep
And when she woke up
He was there for her
With her as her
And she cried every time she sang to him, with
him, for him
Glorious as he is, was, will be
She fell to her knees behind the doors
She raised her hands up
Cried loud, more
She short, tall, stands up
Ask for more
She's changed from before
Her posture like elms

Her legs like runners
Her eyes blasted in light
She sees in front of her
Self I am
Freed one, freedom
She's a part of history now
His story, now.

So I Wrote- Story of Spring

Sunshine set its light on night
And winds bent their arms
Around
Swarms of bumble bees
Bent crooked knees
Hearts, mind at ease
Feeling pretty, pleased
By
Lovers' lane
Memories of dimmed war-houses
Left men somewhat insane
But none of them to blame
Since they were quick-stepped men children
Of single mothers
Who smothered them
Left the girls in a world
All their own
Cyclical movements to the throne
Chills within movements of their own
Family grew and grew
Slid to home
Base encased by lies
Life struggles, present passed by
Future, a dream
Captured in scenes
Unseen
Emote heat from
Wrath of mind

To keep my peace
I wrote a rhyme
Never to be dead...again
So I wrote to cover all visions
Hidden deep within
Flies flew far away
Buzzing
Nothing left.

HENRY WESTRAY JR.

Henry Westray Jr. Is often referred to as the Renaissance man par excellence, as he has had successful careers in several professional fields in the U.S.A. and abroad. Born in Baltimore, he returned to his native town after living in Africa. While he likes to write poetry and short stories, his background includes work as a program director, assistant professor, author, television host, family therapist and workshop presenter.

Henry has a BA in Sociology from Morgan State University and a Master of Social Work from Bryn Mawr College. In addition, he did an internship at the Harvard School of Public Health, Violence Prevention Program.

Henry has held faculty appointments at the University of Lagos in Nigeria, Morgan State University and Howard University. Prior to retiring from public service in 2012, he held the position of Director of Youth Suicide Prevention for the State of Maryland. Under his leadership, he was instrumental in establishing and subsequently chairing the first Governor's Commission on Suicide Prevention in Maryland. During his tenure, Maryland led the nation in reducing the rate of suicide among youth, according to an analysis of data from the Centers for Disease Control and Prevention (CDC). He helped drift and served as the Director of Maryland's three year, $1.3 million, Federal Garrett Lee Smith Grant. In his role within the state government, he led the charge to develop the nation's first decentralized telephone line, the Maryland Youth Crisis Hotline (1-800-422-0009), which opened in 1990. The Federal hotline 1 800-273-TALK was based on the Maryland hotline model. He was also part of a panel of the U.S. Surgeon General, David Satcher, M.D., to write "Call to Action", A National Report on Suicide, published in 1999. He was subsequently invited to attend the first White House conference on suicide prevention, chaired by the second lady, Tipper Gore.

Henry's poems and health-related articles have been published in several local publications in Maryland. He was honored to have been commissioned to write Faces of Fear for the Harvard University Field Notes Journal. His poetry "Boxes" appears in the book "Sixteen", recently published (2021) by The Loch Raven Review. For over two decades, he has been a member of the Black Male Book Club, The Literary Ten. He is also a member of the Black Writers Guild and two other writer's groups. Interesting side: He has been a judge for four State Miss America Pageants, he likes to write original quotes, his most recent quote being, "Dreams are themes that we build our days to welcome".

He has also hosted a local cable show, "Poetic Rhythm", which won a Cameo prize. As a host, he interviewed stars such as Wil Smith, Jada Pinkett-Smith, Pattie Labelle, Jasmine Guy and Mariette Hartley to "name drop a few".

Henry continues to write poems and short stories and feels blessed by the opportunities he is given. He is truly touched by the many awards he has received for his professional and pro bono work. He hopes you will enjoy the collection of poems. He is currently working on a collection of poems that he hopes to release next year. He gave thanks to those whose wings he borrowed to fly beyond his dreams. He can be reached by email at blkspirit1@comcast.net.

<u>A Slice of Heaven</u>

I know it's just a filling on top of crust it's true
But every time I see one I go into a stew
My heart begins a beating my lips begin to ache
I've even been known to eat a few
Just before they bake
The smell is so inviting
The taste oh so divine
I only have one problem
It goes right on my behind
I know this all sounds crazy
A passion I can't deny
For when I die my last request will be for
A warm, smooth, honey colored
Vanilla creamed drenched nutmeg
Melted, cinnamon soaked
Butter baked, sweet potato pie!

I Know Why the Willow Weep

On this rainy winter's day
The lifeless willow outside my window
Also seems to be in mourning
As rain drops slowly fall
On freeze-dried branches
I wonder if the willow tree
Will fall victim to winter's
Icy death-nail

I remember the day
We moved in together
I was so touched when you
Insisted that we plant a willow tree
It soon become a beautiful
Yet calming focal point
Of our front lawn
But it was you who so lovingly
Nurtured that tree
Until it grew lustrous and strong
As I reminisce…
I fondly remember when as kids we played
Under that sleepy old wiry willow tree
Perched high on a hill
Next to a lake behind my parent's house
For year's everyone thought
Because that tree arched so very far over the
Lake… it would eventually fall in
That was some twenty-five years ago

And wouldn't you know
That tree is still there leaning strong
It was also once
Our secret cool oasis
From the day's hot summer's sun
Under that tree we laughed
At our silly juvenile jokes
And played hide and seek
Chasing each other around the lawn
In and out of our tree retreat
Until we were totally exhausted

Before having lunch under the tree
Needing to be refreshed from the heat
Well away from curious eyes
We swam naked in the cool clear lake
Feeling renewed we dressed
And sat on a blanket under
The willow's long ancient looking branches
So hungry that we attacked my straw picnic
Basket filled with goodies ready to eat
At times the willow's thin branches seemed
To sway with our spirit as if it
Was happy to share its space
For lunch we ate tuna sandwiches
And had our fill of my mother's
Renowned southern sweet-iced tea
And her legendary sweet potato pie for dessert
With our stomachs full
We felt like we were on an intimate date at

Some swanky five-star downtown restaurant
One day…we dared to carve love notes
To each other on the trunk of the Willow
Notching into the tree's bark
Words of our love inside
A huge heart with Cupid's
Arrow symbolically piercings it with love
Afraid tree squatters would someday learn
That the notes we were between two teen males
So…notched fake names in the tree's bark
Today...alone as I look through my window
Rain droplets continue their slow descent
Down the willow's green elongated branches
Before finally hitting solid earth
Now, I know why the willow weeps
You see… it misses you and me at play
Under its wings

Colored Day on Buddy Deane
"Hair Sprayed Over"

I tell you…this was no rap scene
And there's a "Black Out" on my screen
Was there too much Afro Sheen?
'Cus we can dance on a balance beam
Banned from T.V. Hill's dance team

Colored Day on Buddy Deane

No mixing of the race
Afraid they'd catch a little trace
Those sponsors you'd have to face
Maybe America could not erase
A black teen dancing with your white daughter
Disrupting the whole world order
The Klan would raid the T.V. Hill border
So they gave us our own day
Being forced to find a way
To let us dance and shine
Stop kicking our behind
No more waiting in line

Only once a month the time
No race mixing and all would be fine

Colored Day on Buddy Deane

White mothers started to scream
Doesn't the KKK run supreme?
Could this all be a bad dream?
Only white kids should be seen!

And just where was Buddy Deane?
Well…he was no Mr. Clean
They say, he held the torch that lit the
cross-burner's flame
Now, let's all go out and be seen

'Cuz it's Colored Day on Buddy Deane

(Baltimore native, John Waters wrote and directed the 1988 Movie Hair Spray. The movie, later turned into a play, was based on the Buddy Deane Show, a Baltimore based white's only teen T.V. dance show.)

Dusty Road

I've known dusty roads
Or is it that too many dusty roads
Have known me
Dust storms have often veiled my view
From roadblocks to climb over
Slide under, go around or just push through

The fresh blush of youth has nearly gone
Entombed on ancient roads I've traveled on
With loving souls now gone dust to dust
Too many caught in dust storms
Where they lay to rust
My soul must confess
That I've had a dusty time or two
But my restless heart still beats
But just a little less

<u>Faded</u>

My *black suit* is worn
Tattered by the souls I've lost
A patch work of memories slowly fading away
A loose thread here, an unraveled fiber there
Sometimes I wonder what will be left
At the end of the day

Treads are unsewn by a
Sadistic tailor 's demented loom
The soul of my suit fits like a ghostly tomb
Hand woven moments ever so gently doomed

Should I throw my shrouded suit away
Or let it wither slowly on the line

As the wind and sunlight 's prey
What if death should come again my way
In search of another precious life to take

(This poem was written to honor friends lost during the AIDS Pandemic)

Falling in Love

I fell in love today
My heart danced, pranced
And even romanced
Stolen glances walking down the hall
A startling glimpse while shopping in the mall
I flowed and just glowed like a newborn
Blushed and tried to run away
The sightings we shared now everyday
When I looked deep in those eyes
All I could say was hooray
Couldn't believe this romantic me
I was a sight to see
Finally, could trust someone I had ignored
And only sometimes adored from afar
Eyes aglow and who would know
That the one I fell in love with was…me

Finding Joy

Is Joy only for a moment
Or does it last a lifetime through
If your heart is empty
Can I give half my Joy to you
Is Joy found high on a mountain
In a secret hiding place
And if it's been there long enough
Does it even leave a trace
Will you find it resting deep in some
Old abandoned mine
Or will it stagger in at midnight
After that last medicinal glass of wine

Will Joy march in as your savior
When you're old and gray
Or float down in divine order
When you kneel to pray

If you make a joyful noise unto the Lord
Surely joy will come through for you
What if it's GPS is broken
And it can't even get to you

Does Joy have a color
Or is it crystal clear
Can you tell when your Joy
Is setting next to you

Will Joy find that working mother
Struggling to keep her child's
Hunger pains at bay
Knowing all awhile her pantry door
Will open empty again today

Is Joy what you feel
When you "come-out" as gay

Should Joy be given first
To those with the highest net worth
Or should all be bathed in fields of Joy
The moment of our birth

Can Joy be captured from the laughter
Of a child at play
And will it linger in a misty moment
Of a love several lifetimes away

I just have one more question
Before I call it a day
Is there even a place for Joy in your heart
During these trying times today

There are so many joy filled questions
Sometimes, the answers seem so few
But there's one thing that's for certain
I know to be joyfully true

I found my Joy today
Just being here with you!

<u>Snowbird</u>

Snowbird can I fly with you
Above the midnight sky
Your soft wings stretch to the heavens
Where I know I need to fly
Days are cold and nights too steep
Save me from this deadly sleep
Cold North winds
Have frozen my lips to stone
Our love is what keeps
My heart beating strong
Snowbird… let's soar through soft silvery clouds
To feel my lover's arms
My world is much s warmer there
Safely sealed from any harm
We'll whisk away through whirling winds and
Weather any storm
Race with doves across bluest skies
Until they run out of notes
To sing their peaceful song
We'll Climb the steepest mountain
Until the air is thin and still
Mourn with weeping willows
And all rivers have had its fill
Just to see lover's heart
Fill with laughter again
And we'll dance with daffodils
Until the earth standstill

<u>The Parade</u>

When I learned I could live without you
I had a parade!
Marched up and down the whole block
I was the Band Leader
The Cheer Leader
I was the whole damn marching band
At six a.m. when the streetlights went out
To my neighbor's riotous applause
I put down my battered baton
Then proudly marched back in house
And bolted the door

The Room

In this room in this space
Sounds of silence were erased
As we journeyed through the seasons of our love
Smiles smiled, laughs laughed and hopes hoped
Hands held, eyes eyed, and kisses kissed
Arms embraced lovingly
Unmasking once silent spaces inside our souls
Shimmering sun shined brightly
Through transom windows
Glistening in the joy of our loving reflection
Summer kitchen smelled of savory spices
And sounds of love songs aglow
Floors seemed to polish themselves
Moving to our heartbeats in stereophonic sounds
Sadly, love was built
On ungraded gilded grounds
In this room in this space
The ceiling leaked when a secret love

Landed on its rafters
The foundation fought to
Shake away all happy eve-afters
Questions questioned, lies lied
And words "war ed"
Truth could not be found
Even in darkened dusty corners
Walls went weak as doors closed tightly
From closets of mistrust
Fueled by a toxic squawking silence
In this room in this space
We danced with distant feet not keeping pace
"Ungraved" emotions ran out of grace
Rage raged, grief grieved, and tears teared
Floors cracked from the weight of weighted fears
Bedroom eyes sealed shut
Hurricanes of hate painted our view
From pain pulsating in our gut
Washing away well-worn roads to each other
In this room in this space
Our love ended in this place
As fragile footsteps found footing
To heal in other rooms

The Gift

May your days soar with inspiration

Drenched in dazzling domes of hope

Seasoned with sun beams of delight

Let your nights be blessed

Bathed in warm seas

Of sleepy time dreams

Covered by a soft peaceful blanket

Patiently stitched and quilted

By grandma's loving hand

From patches of sacred bouquets

For a quiet restful night

<u>When Heroes Fall</u>

When heroes fall can we really hear the sound?
My Child:
The sound is there although you may not hear it, for it silently sings in spiritual scales sent from heaven. Please remember that this silence is still in rhythm with your soul. One note is missing, but your loved one still sings with you. Their muted voice embraces your spirit, although they are gone.

When heroes fall do storm clouds cover mountains with the strength of a hurricane, announcing their passing?
My Beloved:
We are those mountains, and your tears are hurricanes of sorrow sent to heal your heart.

When heroes fall how do we know we can go on?
Honorable One:
When heroes fall life silences your soul in stillness for just a moment. This muted world allows you to take a fresh look at your inner self, fill empty spaces close to your heart, and to reexamine the world for new insight and direction. It is not by accident that the rainbow comes after

the tempest. Your loss is that storm, the rainbow is the sacred signal guiding you to new paths set before you. Look for the rainbow in loving eyes in bloom around you. Breathe in those flowers that speak to your soul and to your laughter as a child. Although heroes die, their passing warm sacred spaces to season your return home. The loving memory of their earthly words and deeds will still be there to nurture the hero in you.

<u>When Seashells Speak</u>

Soulful sounds lie silent through seasons simmering in seashells
Just listen
Observe oceans of mighty moments marooned in muses of mermaids
Just listen
Cascading cool currents catch clouds of rain running through rivers,
brooks, and bays
Just listen
Testy tides tease shores with wisdom
As scorched sands shiver when waters approach their dunes
Just listen
Which way will this mighty current take us?
Will we be shattered to secret shadows of the deep?
Or be bathed on seashores by the sun
Only Seashells know the secrets
Just Listen

Winter

My fear of Winter went away
Blustery breezes did not brittle my bones
Or crystalize my blood to a frozen glacier red
Ash-layered skies did not languor
The heat of my heart
Nor did a Winter's wind whisper my death
But signaled a sojourn to retreat to the soul
Where frigid voices, from the summer's sun
Whispered, that icy havens only heal
From the heat of a loving heart
Are revealed in the radiance of a smile
Revel in the warmth of a hello
Rest in the rapture of a loving ritual
Riveted in time
Only then will icicles of fear fade
Kindling glances of hope
Winter is for wondering beyond windows

Nadia Stokes, Henry Westray Jr., & Joslyn Caldwell

Imagining through looking glasses
For touching celestial secrets
And seasoning ourselves for spring

JOSLYN CALDWELL

I was born and raised in California where I grew up in a single parent home. I found my love for writing at the age of 12. My first poem was called "A Woman Weeps", it was a piece that spoke on how women suffer in silence. I fell in love with writing after that and went on to recite poems in church. Through high school and college, I always made sure to take a Creative Writing class at some point. My work displays my thoughts, feelings and humor while often showcasing my battle with dyslexia. Now I am a mother and a woman of a certain age, I have grown and evolved over the years, but writing is still a passion that I adore.

The Loss of Her

Abcdefghi. . .123456
Let me be me
Who is me that I struggle to be.
Who me who I see or rather what I attempt to believe
Couldn't possibly be me.
Someone ring an alarm, send me a text
This dream I sleep can't be the reality I so do seek
Or live.
She left me. . .

Abcdefghijkl. . .345678. . .

Ruined by prosperity
Congratulated for failure but continuous success
Because you have to fail to succeed but maybe
You succeed to fail.
She died without me. . .

Resentment for the truth but
Happiness to the lies that blind
How is that what this world lives for.
Pleased to the blinding ladders of success
A rock, a pill, some leaves
Who hasn't made a living off of someone else
Trying to escape sorrow.
Blind faith, blind reality, blind to what is an illusion
For someone else.

My planet is not mother earth
My planet is the carpet that lies beneath my feet.
For just like war,
You disturb my planet
I…will kill
Metaphorically, of course.

So many nights that I will never spend alone.
She is in the stars
And much like those nights spent on my mother's old car
I observe her much like she observes.
We gaze, I gaze on the beauty that is now in the sky
That was once a vision of her before me.

Every time I cry out for her

The taste of sweet peach cobbler hits my lips
And I escape to the times when I could smell it
As soon as her door opened.
She was my connection to reality
Without her I have lost the reflection of me.

The time to move on is not now
Because the reality that surrounded me
Still exists much like it did
When she left me. . .

<u>Commentary on Ignorance</u>

I am desperate
Desperate for happiness
For innocent thoughts
For members of the male species
That want to have mind relations
Instead of just wanting to abuse my uterus
I want motivation
To succeed in life
Being a nobody sucks after a while
I intertwine with the air
Oxygen is my companion
They say call on the Lord, He is your friend
Well, shit, what's his number
Maybe we can chat sometime
Over some Lipton and finga sandwiches
They say go out
Don't focus on being alone
Meet people
With what money and what car
I'm broke
Besides who says that I'll meet
People who care about
What kind of
Person I am or pretend to be
Give me paper and a pen
At least I know then
The for real
The fact that the words are meaningful
And honest

Seed of The Invisible Man

The hope I had for a better present day
Is now replaced with the desperation
For a simple tomorrow.
My heart no longer cries
It bleeds
Mentally I have been broken down to
The goofy and unfocused little girl I once was.
I can't stop thinking about him.
The man I was supposed to call father
The man that was supposed to have all the answers
Better yet. . .
I was supposed to be a "daddy's girl".
My mind continues to wander, and I think to myself
Friends? What the fuck is that?
They all I have either turned they back on me
Or treated me so bad
I turned my back on them
I'm frustrated
I'm mad
I can't do this anymore. . .
The metal shines in my face as I sit at the kitchen table
Everyone has gone to bed
And yet here I am with a full plate sitting under the light
Alone.
My heart begins to race
My mind unclear of what I'm about to
Frankly I just want the pain to end.
I pick up the steak knife. . .

Hold up to my neck
And with one shift motion. . .
It's over
As my face falls into the plate,
I mumble into the steak and potatoes
"It's over."

<u>Does This Makes Sense to Anyone But Me?</u>

Wandering thru life
Trying to find a place to fit
Spiritual growth,
I lost my path.
Emotional growth,
Expired when I was 14.
Homeless constantly,
Mentally vacant,
Sometimes I float thru crowds,
Feeling like a seed of the invisible man.
Confusion surrounds my being.
Today is tomorrow,
Tomorrow is yesterday,
Last week was an hour ago.
But ask me what happened 15 minutes ago,
And I can't remember.
Ask me what's goin' on right now,
And I'll lose all presence of time.

I wonder why I exist
Is this life even for me?
I have dreams of escaping the dark shadows of failure
That seem to haunt me.
I blame my exposure to harsh reality on no one.
My pain is expressed thru frustration and silence.
Rage and heartache the only true emotions
I have felt in a long time.
I know death will reach me soon. . .

<u>Existence</u>

I have no face.
I have no place in time
Wandering through the sea of people
I am an element
In this place called earth
With each step
I change the outlook on nature
That much more
I have no spirit
I follow what others believe that seem to suit me
I have no eyes
The things I seem to see are just a figment of my imagination
I have no sense of reality
The things I have been through can't be real
I have no desire
Because putting forth effort is
Just not something I'm interested in
Doing at this point in time
I have no self-esteem because if I did that last statement
Would have never crossed my mind.
I have no concept of time
Endless nights, sleep filled days consume me
I have no true understanding
If I did then this poem wouldn't exist

Inquiries of a Pandemic Mind

Give me my roses without thorns
Criticism without construction
Leads to the abolishment of my ambition
Love me for who I am striving to be
Rather than objectifying the person who
You thought me to be
They say love is a battlefield
But I never declared war. . .
What is the point in an army
When the only soldier is me
Truthfully, I cannot see the reflection
You have created
I can only be the person in the mirror
But I am lost now,
Because I have no recognition
The conflicting situation has left me
In a position of internal despair
Wondering if the resolution is near
Praying for something
That is not even there
Finding peace seems so unfair
Give me something
Because the nothing is torture
Or is the anguish more in the fact that
It is just another Tuesday
Whether you are here or not.

<u>My Superman</u>

Melodies play in my head
With the sound of your voice
Your laugh brings
A warmth inside me that I can't even
Begin to explain.
Your strength is something
That I will forever admire.
My experience with you
Is something I will treasure for a lifetime
I desire your mental stimulation
For the simple fact
Your wisdom on life
Surpasses mine.
Learning more about you
Has made me come to realize
That you have exceeded my expectations
Of what I always thought a real man was
And at times I am intimidated.
Truthfully, I need you.
I want no one but you
I desire your heart
Because in mine you can never be replaced
The life I have lived
The turmoil I have been through I had honestly given up
Never thought I would find happiness
Never thought I would have that
Knight in shining armor
But yet here you are.
And if I have my way here you will remain.

Lies of a Broken Beating Muscle

Lies of a Broken Heart
Four years
Four years, Three times incarcerated
And by his side I stood. . .
Drip
He loves me no matter what
Drip
I'm the only one in his life
Drip
It's me…not him
Drip
Mary J. is right love IS all we need
Drip
If it's meant to be we will find away
Splat. . .
As I collapse, I realize,
Through the fuzzy haze
He is not my knight
He is not my soul-mate
He is an illusion
I made because of my depression
And as I lay here
I hope I don't die
From his ignorance and lies.

<u>Thoughts of an Open Mind</u>

True prosperity
Is essential to be content
In life of solitude
Growing in mystery
Pleasing to the eye
But deceiving to the heart
Nature's beauty has
No continuous form
Life's options
Are disappointing
But they satisfy the simple minded
You work so hard to find that special someone
But end up dying alone
Wandering. . .trying to find your god
But after your body has taken
It's last breath
There is no swallowing your pride
And admitting you are wrong
Death isn't about facing the truth
But acknowledging it
It is like you don't
Face the fact that most apples are red
You acknowledge it
Death is a red apple
Simple to see
But to take it apart
You reveal so much more.

Untitled

Dream Me
Dream You
Dream me and you. . .together
For real life is our separator
Test and trials I have put you through
But my words confessed
That I love you
For the sun moved me
While the moon caressed you
I rolled in the sand of the desert
While you played in the snow of the Alps
I love you but not enough
To be humane to my own feelings
I never denied them in my heart
Or in my conscious thought
But subconsciously I played the fool
Never showing my feelings thru action
But by mouth
By mouth was easy. . .maybe too easy
Action was the challenge,
I was never truly ready for
Doubt of you in my head
Caused some hypocritical, maybe unbelievable
Things to transpire
So as a result of my stupidity
The only way we can be together
Is in my dreams
One question is in my heart

That I will never ask you
If my love remained
Today, tomorrow, forever
Do you think one day you could love me too?

<u>Word Strength</u>

If I say it with a smirk
I'm being playful
If I say it with a smirk and
A raised eyebrow
I'm being evil
If I say it with a giggle
I'm being bashful
If I say it with a tear in my eye
I'm being fearful
The depth of a word
Can be taken
To so many realms of contemplation
Redundancy
Can diminish
Repetition
Can entrap the masses
The strength of a word
Is not in definition
But in the intention.

Mood Ring

The passion of purple
It feels so mysterious
But yet so divine
I want to taste it
I want to wrap myself in it
Let it caress my mind
The warmth of orange
Leaves my skin sun-kissed
Eases my fears and lets me dance in bliss
The fury of red
I can't sit still
I pace back and forth,
forth and back
To the point my rage burns my path into the carpet
Like the markings of a dropped cigarette
The sadness of blue
Tears soak my pillow
Feels like I used it to float away in the ocean
Feels like the weight of the world on my shoulders
Feels like the heaviness of my heart
Feels like I wish I could be...
The pureness of white
All over again…

An Expression of Lost

Climb into my skin
See my life
My birth to present
Realize my struggles are real
The truth I know

The lies that consume me
Harsh realities that teach me
I'm blessed to have knowledge
I'm cursed to have knowledge
Secrets told; whispers yelled

A slap in the face only stings
When you're sober
Not a runaway love
But continuously running from love
Running from. . .
Well just running

Because walking away hurts too much
Live in chaos but still step into the world with a smile
Weakness is never to be shown but embraced
And made into a strength
My thoughts are like leaves on a windy fall day
Scattered. . .

Rainbow Brite, Fraggle Rock, Thunder Cats,
I remember those

Not for their greatness in time
But because those were the times
I smiled the most
I laughed the most
They mark a past time that makes this time seem
Lost.

OUR COLLABORATIVE PIECE ON COVID

What do you mean there is no more toilet paper?
Why are you asking if I left the country?
I can't even leave my house?

A part of what was

To gather what is

To breathe in air

Covid-19, it's been said that if there is a number behind your name It
tells you how many reincarnations you've been granted

Of one who lived and still dreams

Stilled dreams

You've murdered millions of good folks world-wide
Who dared to glimpse into your murderous Medusa eyes?

You mean death has been a guest at my table
This whole time?

From finish to start we were made to be

Still

Growing angst for some
Including my next-door neighbor's daughter Debbie
Who we loved dearly for she was such a joyous loving child

With a kind-hearted manner

I feel like a walking panic attack...
This came from bats?
Next they'll be saying that the swine flu came from Mickey Mouse

As a famous mafia hitman once said
"I murder each client multiple times
So, they never have to worry about being my next crime"
Covid, you'll be glad to know, that I've only placed the best
And most painfully cruel schemes in my Covid torture chest

Don't you dare sneeze
And you better not cough

Deepened faith for others

Both in a river with rough waters

Swimming, floating, drowning

Borders

Why is this woman standing so close to me
Is this what 28 days later was talking about?
Why has no one still told me why there is no toilet paper

Covid, I guess you have no mercy for a person's age
Or their worth inside, you'll just kill anyone from nine to ninety-five

Will my children ever get to be outside again
Will hazmat suits be on clearance at Target for $16.99?

Hope together, gathered to gather parts that were before

Again

Breath out

Masks down

Grandpa was such a wise old man
Who had pride in family, shared his wisdom and strong faith in God
In dreams, I still hear his gentle voice
Just before I abruptly wake up crying

Pray

Breathe

In

Soar

Wait, where is my mask?

Covid, I hate you and wish death to every life you took
But I just remembered something my grandpa once said
In the Lord's eyes, "Both hatred and revenge are twins of the same
ungodly sin."

If you don't die by my hands, let the scientists do you in

Will the world ever be "normal"?

NUBIAN VOICES UNMASKED:
The Elements of a Poem

<u>Together, a part</u>
Nadia Stokes

A part of what was
To gather what is
To breathe in air
Of one who lived and still dreams
Stilled dreams
Awakened by blocked faces
Thoughts
Missing parts
From finish to start we were made to be
Still
Growing angst for some
Deepened faith for others
Both in a river with rough waters
Swimming, floating, drowning
Borders
Yet still here
And more than before
Hope together, gathered to gather parts that were before
Again
Breath out
Masks down
Pray
Breathe
In.
Soar.

<u>Nineteen Ways to Kill COVID-19</u>
"Confessions of a serial Covid killer"

Henry Westray

It's said, that if there is a number behind your name
It tells you how many reincarnations you've been granted
So Covid-19, I have to kill you 19 times
That way I'll be sure you're truly dead
As a famous mafia hit man once said
"I murder each client multiple times
So, they never have to worry they'll be my next crime"
Covid, you'll be glad to know, that I've only placed the best
And most painfully cruel schemes in my Covid torture chest
Since you've murdered millions of good folks world-wide
Who dared to glimpse into your Medusa killer eyes
Including my next-door neighbor's daughter Debbie
Who we loved dearly for she was a joyous loving child
With a contagious warm kind-hearted manner
How could you put a mere child in your Covid deadly ring
When she was only nine years old and couldn't fight a thing
I've been sad and full of rage, since she passed away last Spring
From your dreaded Covid hell
And by the way, she was the Wilson's only child
Who they called their blessed miracle everyday
I guess you have no mercy for a person's age
Or consider their worth inside
You'll kill anyone from nine to ninety-five
For ninety-five was the age you murdered my grandpa Fred
One morning, I was the one who found him dead in bed
Grandpa was such a wise old man
Who shared his wisdom, pride in family, and his faith in God

We loved to hear him sing with such love and devotion
As he so passionately sang on the Church Sunday Choir
In dreams, I still hear his gentle voice
Just before I abruptly wake up crying
For both of my loved ones, I'll stab you
19 times with a pitch-fork dead in your RNA
Then I'll cut off your protein spiked heads with a rusty nail
You'll be in such pain you'll beg me for death
After that, you'll be my target practice round after round
Until only a tiny spore of you can be found
I'll then pound what's left into a snake filled swampy ground
Pull you out and put you on a stove on high flame
Just to watch you sizzle and fry
I'll have our local drug pusher, overdose any left-over hope
I'll crawl into your most pleasant dreams
And choke you until I hear your tonsils scream
Next, I'll disguise your best love
And force them to look deep in your eyes
After you've murdered them with a thrill
Only then will I tell you; you had just killed
Your one and only best friend

Well, my grandpa's now in God's hands
No longer will I ever feel his joy again
Or stay up late with him on Saturday nights
'till Eyewitness News begins

By the way, I know I said I'd list 19 ways to kill and only listed nine
'Cuz I just remembered something my grandpa once said

In the Lord's eyes, "Both hatred and revenge are twins of the same
ungodly crime"
To honor Grandpa and his love for all mankind
I'll throw the next ten ways to kill you in God's hands

COVID Tribulations

Joslyn Caldwell

What do you mean there's no toilet paper?
Why are you asking me if I left the country?
I can't even leave my house
Don't sneeze
Don't cough
This came from a bat. . .
What were they doing with the bat
I could have had this over a year ago
And didn't even know it
You mean death has been a guest at my table
This whole time?!
Where is my mask
Damnit, I feel like lint is now the new oxygen
Lord please don't let my nose run
Why has no one still told me why there was
No toilet paper
Why is this woman standing so close to me
I feel like a walking panic attack
Is this what 28 days later was talking about?
This year's school supply list
Face masks and sanitizer
What happened to markers and paper
Will my kids ever get to go outside
Will I ever be comfortable to have
Seasonal allergies again
Will red dye number 6 be added to the list
Of possible causes
Will the world ever be "Normal"

Or will hazmat suits be on clearance
at Target For $16.99 next week?

ACKNOWLEDGMENTS

We are honored to have our work presented in this Anthology and to finally give birth to the book, Nubian Voices Unmasked. There is an old African saying, "When Spider Webs Unite… they can tie up a lion". We'd like to honor the strong web of folk who helped us ferociously tie up this lion of a book. Foremost, we'd like to thank our many friends and family for their prayers, encouragement, and support. A special thanks goes out to Mr. Tyrone M. Eddins Jr., who came up with the idea of publishing this book, taking a chance on highlighting work by three relatively unknown Black Writers. Throughout the process of pulling this book together, he has been truly committed to making these pages sing with our own voices. He has also been an inspiration, guiding us safely through the forest land of publishing. For this we say, thanks again! Having three very talented but different writers work together on this book has had its ups and downs, and sometimes even seemed to go sideways at times. But we always came back together, even stronger because of our united vision to unmask our creative voices through these pages.

We'd like to end with another African proverb, "Even straight trees have crooked roots". We trust that the crooked roots that nourished the richness of our words on these sacred pages, also touch your heart. Thanks again to all who made this journey possible. Enjoy!

*African proverbs are borrowed from "unknown authors".